ODD
ONE
OUT

The Devilish Quiz for History Lovers

Paul Sullivan

First published 2014

The History Press
The Mill, Brimscombe Port
Stroud, Gloucestershire, GL5 2QG
www.thehistorypress.co.uk

Reprinted 2015

British Library Cataloguing in Publication Data.
A catalogue record for this book is available from the British Library.

ISBN 978 0 7509 5572 0

Typesetting and origination by The History Press
Printed in Great Britain

Which one of these men is not associated with the potato plant?

Patrick Bellew • Sir Walter Raleigh •
Sir John Hawkins

ANSWER: Bellew is the odd one out, being the first tomato grower, although all three were horticultural pioneers. Raleigh and Hawkins were among the first to grow potatoes.

Patrick Bellew, descendant of Anglo-Norman aristocrats and forebear of later Irish barons and high sheriffs, was the first British person to grow tomatoes (at his family seat in Castletown, County Louth, Ireland, in 1554). They were slow to catch on. John Gerard's best-seller *Herball*, published in 1597, calls tomatoes 'Apples of Love', but notes that 'the whole Plant is of a rank and stinking savour … In Spain and those hot Regions they use to eat the Apples prepared and boiled with pepper, salt, and oil: but they yield very little nourishment to the body, and the same nought and corrupt.'

If you wish to believe the legend, **Sir Walter Raleigh** (1552–1618) was Britain and Ireland's first potato grower. His first crop sprang up in 1589 on his Irish estates at Youghal in County Cork. Raleigh has been credited with introducing the vegetable to Europe, but this is not the case – It was brought over from South America by the Spaniards in the 1570s. One legend even asserts that the first potatoes planted in Ireland were salvaged from the wreck of the Spanish Armada in 1588.

Another story says that seadog **Sir John Hawkins** (1532–95), mastermind of the Elizabethan navy, harvested the first English potatoes in 1565.

Only one of these men associated with Stratford-upon-Avon did not write about the town — but which?

J.B. Priestley • Arthur C. Clarke •
William Shakespeare

ANSWER: All of them lived at some point in Stratford-upon-Avon. William Shakespeare, in spite of being the Bard of Avon, is the only one who never actually wrote about the town.

J.B. Priestley (1894–1984) made fleeting references to the famous town in his non-fiction work, while in 1953 **Arthur C. Clarke** (1917–2008) wrote a short sci-fi story, 'The Curse', set in a post-apocalyptic Stratford. Clarke had served in the RAF, based near the town. The title of his story is a reference to the famous curse on the grave of **William Shakespeare** (1564–1616) in St Mary's church, Stratford (spelling modernised):

Good friend for Jesus' sake forbear
To dig the dust enclosed here.
Blessed be the man that spares these stones,
And cursed be he that moves my bones.

Which of these famous leaders banned moustaches for practical reasons?

Alexander the Great •
Mustafa Kemal Ataturk • Tony Blair

ANSWER: Alexander the Great.

Alexander the Great (356–23 BC) was King of Macedon and a legendary conqueror. His ban on all facial hair applied to the army only, and was for wholly practical reasons, rather than fashion or political statement. He brought in the earliest known version of the military short back and sides. His logic was that hair gave his enemies something to grab during battle. Prior to this decree, men in Greek society had sported long locks and bushy beards. This ushered in the clean-shaven look that enjoyed a renaissance in Ancient Rome, in which only barbarians, philosophers and certain slaves sported facial hair.

Mustafa Kemal Ataturk (1881–1938), Ottoman and Turkish officer and first President of Turkey, banned the moustache in Turkey as a political, secular gesture. During the Ottoman years, all men had worn luxuriant moustaches. As part of his country's post-First World War secularisation, Ataturk shaved his 'tache off, in public, to inspire all Turkish men to do likewise and embrace the secular life. He made the example more pressing by introducing a dress code that banned the growing of Ottoman-style moustaches (the fez being another victim of the stylistic axe).

Tony Blair (1953–) was British prime minister between 1997 and 2007. He banned the moustache in Cabinet meetings in the interests of party image. They just weren't 'New Labour'. He made it known that he did not want to see moustaches on governmental stiff upper lips, although full beards were acceptable.

Which of these cigar-smoking statesmen wasn't actually very fond of cigars?

Winston Churchill • John F. Kennedy • Josef Stalin

ANSWER: Stalin.

Winston Churchill (1874–1965), legendary wartime leader, prime minister, historian, writer and wit, fell in love with Cuban cigars during his stay in Havana in 1885 as a 20-year-old journalist. He claimed that his diet in the early days of his stay revolved around Cuban oranges and cigars. Back home, Churchill tended to smoke the Romeo y Julieta brand, and one called La Aroma de Cuba. He smoked between six and ten a day, and had a ready supply at his home in Chartwell, numbering in the thousands. As one of history's stranger job perks, Churchill used to give his cigar stubs to his gardener, who used them to fill his pipe.

John F. Kennedy (1917–63), famously assassinated US President and enthusiastic cigar smoker, signed the legislation that banned the import of Cuban cigars into the USA. However, before the law came into force he stocked up on the best smokes available. It was a dilemma for the country – Cuban cigars were widely held to be the best on the market, and well worth coughing up for. In the kind of perverseness not seen since the alcohol prohibition laws of the 1920s, the trade embargo made Cuban cigars more popular than ever in the US. It is still not legal to import them, but tourists are allowed to bring back huge stashes for personal consumption.

Josef Stalin (1878–1953), born Iosif Vissarionovich Dzhugashvili, was Soviet Communist Party chairman and dictator. At the Potsdam Conference in 1945 he smoked Cuban cigars in the belief that they would give him a more statesmanlike air than his usual chain-smoked cigarettes. He was not a fan of cigars, however, and his second choice of tobacco inhalation, after Hertsegovina Flor Papirossi cigarettes, was the briar pipe – filled with tobacco taken from the cigarettes. At Potsdam, Winston Churchill told Stalin that a photo of him smoking a 'Churchillian' cigar would 'create an immense sensation – everyone will say it is my influence.'

Which of these famous highwaymen wasn't hanged for robbery?

Claude Du Vall • Captain James Hind •
'Swift Nick' Nevison

ANSWER: James Hind.

Claude Du Vall, aka Dumas (1643–70), a miller's son from Normandy, was the classic dashing highwayman, courteous to ladies and never resorting to violence. His favourite haunts were between Islington and Highgate. Ladies were said to have cried and swooned at his Tyburn execution. Flamboyant to the last, he placed the rope around his neck and jumped to his death. Charles II was one of his fans, and wanted him reprieved, but judge Sir William Morton refused to listen.

Captain James Hind (c. 1616–52), from Chipping Norton in Oxfordshire, was hanged, drawn and quartered for treason. A Royalist in the Civil War, he turned highwayman in order to rob Parliamentarians. He successfully mugged John Bradshaw, President of the High Court of Justice, during the trial of King Charles I and, with fellow felon Thomas Allen, he attempted to rob Oliver Cromwell. The hold-up was unsuccessful and Allen was captured, although Hind escaped. When Cromwell eventually caught up with him in 1652, he was charged with treason because of his Royalist sympathies. The charges of highway robbery paled in contrast, and he met his grisly end at Worcester.

Nick Nevison (c. 1639-84), born at Wortley in Yorkshire, was arrested in Sandal Magna hear Wakefield and hanged at York. It was Nevison who rode from London (Gads Hill in Kent, actually) to York to establish an alibi – not Dick Turpin. Charles II, clearly something of a highwayman fan, gave him the 'Swift Nick' title, to celebrate the deed. It was author William Harrison Ainsworth who transferred the feat to Turpin in his novel *Rookwood*. It's possible that neither man actually made the legendary journey – it may have been the otherwise obscure highwayman Samuel Nicks, and the king may have been referring to 'Swift Nicks'.

Which of these three German spies was the last man to be executed at the Tower of London?

Haicke Janssen • Josef Jakobs • Fernando Buschmann

ANSWER: Josef Jakobs.

Haicke Janssen (1886–1915) was a Dutchman caught spying on English seaports in the guise of a cigar salesman, along with his colleague in espionage, Willem Johannes Roos. Under interrogation, the men betrayed a scant knowledge of cigars. London newspapers reported Janssen's death in 1915: 'On 30 July there was a scene in the Tower of London which for grimness was never surpassed during the war. In the early dawn Janssen was led forth to face the firing party. His iron nerve, which had not deserted him throughout, held good to the finish and he died as he had lived, a brave man.'

Josef Jakobs (1898–1941) had parachuted into England on a spying mission, but broke his ankle as he left the aeroplane on 31 January 1941. He landed at Ramsey in Huntingdonshire and was overpowered by the local Home Guard. He was carrying £500 sterling, some forged papers, a radio and a German sausage – the trickiest piece of evidence to argue away. He was shot by firing squad, seated in a Windsor chair, on 15 August 1941.

Fernando Buschmann (1890–1915) was another of the eleven spies executed during the First World War. His gaolers granted his last wish, allowing him to play his violin on the night before the execution. He ended with a mournful piece by Pagliacci, kissed the violin and gave it to one of the gaol warders, whose daughter was a violinist. He faced death – without a blindfold – on 19 September 1915.

There were three conflagrations called the Great Fire of London. London Bridge survived only one of them. Which one?

1135 • 1215 • 1666

ANSWER: 1666.

1135: This Great Fire started on the bridge itself (or in the home of Sheriff of London Gilbert Beckett, father of the famously murdered Thomas Beckett, according to other sources). The blaze fed mercilessly on the wooden medieval city, destroying pretty much everything in the vicinity of the bridge, Cannon Street, Ludgate Hill, Fleet Street and the eastern end of Strand.

1212: This one was also known as the Great Fire of Southwark. The church of St Mary Overie (on the site of the modern Southwark Cathedral) was the first major casualty, and London Bridge followed soon after. It had been rebuilt in stone following the 1135 conflagration, but the timber-framed houses all perished. King John is said to have ordered the construction of these buildings so that their rents would cover the cost of bridge maintenance. Many people had rushed onto the bridge, either to cross the river and assist in fire-fighting, or to escape from the flames. Either way, they perished along with the wooden buildings. The bridge lay in semi-ruin for several decades afterwards.

1666: A fire in 1633 had destroyed forty-two of the buildings that formerly lined London Bridge, at its northern side. These were not replaced in a hurry, which unwittingly created a firebreak – when the 1666 flames approached the bridge from the north, they were disappointed to find no old, dry timber buildings to feed them.

Which of these three bears, all famous London Zoo residents, was named after its keepers?

Winnie • Brumas • Pipaluk

ANSWER: Brumas.

Winnie, an American black bear, was named after Winnipeg in Canada. She was brought to the zoo in 1914 by Canadian Harry Colebourn, a vet and soldier with the Royal Canadian Army Veterinary Corps. He smuggled her into the country as an unofficial regimental mascot. When A.A. Milne and his son Christopher Robin visited the zoo, the boy was entranced by Winnie. The rest is history. The fictional bear Winnie the Pooh first appeared in print in 1924 and Winnie died ten years later, on 12 May 1934.

Brumas the polar bear was named after her two keepers – Bruce Smith and Sam Morton (the latter name reversed). Born on 27 November 1949, she was the first polar bear to be reared in a British zoo. She was an immediate media star – attendance figures in the early 1950s reached 3 million a year, a figure that has never been exceeded. She died on 17 May 1958.

The polar bear **Pipaluk**, meaning 'little one' in the Inuit language, was born at London Zoo on 1 December 1967. Pipaluk's parents Sam and Sally had been named after their keeper Sam Morton (of Brumas fame – see above) and his fiancée Sally. In 1985 Pipaluk was made homeless, after the closure of London Zoo's Mappin Terraces, where all the bears had lived. He moved to Dudley Zoo, and then to Katowice Zoo in Poland in 1989, where he died a year later.

Three kings associated with wolves — but which one was actually thought to be a werewolf?

King John • King Edward I • King James I

ANSWER: King John.

King John (1166–1216) is said to wander the countryside as a werewolf. One of his hunting grounds is Runnymede, site of the famous meeting between king and barons in 1215 that led to the signing of the Magna Carta. The oddest part of the legend is that John only became a werewolf after his death, a possibly unique variation on lycanthropy. It was also said that his family, the Anjous, were generally an impious and black magic-dabbling lot.

King Edward I (1239–1307) was, during his reign (from 1272), an exterminator of wolves. He ordered the total slaughter of the species in England, and employed a dedicated wolf hunter, Peter Corbet. The main battlegrounds were on the Welsh borders, Gloucestershire, Herefordshire, Worcestershire, Shropshire and Staffordshire. Most of the animals were trapped and destroyed rather than hunted on horseback or with wolfhounds. The last wolf in England was cornered and speared in the reign of Henry VII in the late fifteenth century, although legend mentions monstrous specimens still roaming Cornwall thirty-three years later.

King James VI of Scotland (1566–1625) wasn't a werewolf, but he wrote about them. In 1597 (before he became James I of England in 1603), he mentioned werewolves in his witchcraft-busting manual *Demonologie*. He proposed that lycanthropy, if it existed, was a natural medical condition: 'if any such thing has been I take it to have proceeded but of a natural superabundance of melancholie'.

What links the nicknames of the three British kings in each row?

Ethelred II • John • George III

Richard I • William I of Scotland • Henry I

Sweyn Forkbeard • Richard III • Edward I

ETHELRED II · JOHN · GEORGE III

They all had derogatory nicknames: Ethelred the Unready (uncounselled); John Lackland; and George the Mad.

RICHARD I · WILLIAM I OF SCOTLAND · HENRY I

They all had nicknames referring to lions: Richard the Lionheart on account of his bravery; William the Lion, on account of his power and ferocity; and Henry the Lion of Justice, a thumbs-up for his sense of law and order (the same nickname also being applied to Henry II).

SWEYN FORKBEARD · RICHARD III · EDWARD I

They all had nicknames referring to their appearance: Sweyn Forkbeard (son of King Harald Bluetooth of Denmark and father of King Cnut of England), named after his fashionable facial hair; Richard Crouchback on account of his physical shape; and Edward Longshanks, a nickname referring to his great height.

What links the names of the three British kings in each row?

?

William II • William III • Kenneth III of Scotland

Alfred • Cnut (Canute) • Malcolm III of Scotland

Eadweard (son of King Alfred) • Edgar II • Henry III

WILLIAM II · WILLIAM III · KENNETH III OF SCOTLAND

They all had names involving colours: William Rufus (red); William of Orange; and Kenneth the Brown.

ALFRED · CNUT (CANUTE) · MALCOLM III OF SCOTLAND

They were the only British kings to earn the nickname 'Great' – Malcolm was 'Canmore', meaning Great Chieftain (commonly mistranslated as 'big head').

EADWEARD (SON OF KING ALFRED) · EDGAR II · HENRY III

They all had nicknames referring to age: Eadweard the Elder; Edgar Ætheling (meaning young prince); and Henri le Jeune Roi (meaning young king).

Each of these three towns was famous for a sport — but what was the sport? (And which was the only one not to celebrate it with an annual festival?)

Wokingham • Tutbury • Stamford

ANSWER: Bull baiting. Wokingham is the only one that didn't have an annual bull-running festival.

Wokingham never staged bull running, but it was one of the last places in Britain to ban bull baiting. Formerly a regular spectacle on the streets of the town, the blood sport was restricted to once a year in 1822 following the first Cruelty to Animals Act. The excuse for the surviving baiting was that it provided beef for the poor at Christmas. In this guise it lingered until the practice was finally banned outright by an Act of Parliament in 1835.

Tutbury was famous for its bull running. A seventeenth-century ballad celebrating Robin Hood mentions that the famous outlaw married Clorinda, 'the queen of the shepherds', at Tutbury, during the bull-running festival. The sport was banned in 1778 after a man was gored to death by the bull.

Stamford's annual November bull running was a defining feature of the town. The climax of the chase was the 'bridging', in which the bull was forced to jump off a bridge into the River Welland, after which it was baited with dogs. Even when the sport was banned by Parliament in 1835, the townsmen continued the tradition. In 1838 a joint force of dragoons and Metropolitan police had to intervene to prevent a bull being run through the streets. Many bystanders were injured, and several arrests were made. In 1839 a bull was released once again, but was impounded by police, who then had to prevent the 4,000-strong crowd from liberating it. They succeeded, and the tradition was dead at last.

What links these three contemporaries?

James Scott, 1st Duke of Monmouth
• Henry FitzRoy, 1st Duke of Grafton •
Charles FitzCharles, 1st Earl of Plymouth

DIEU ET · MON · DROIT.

ANSWER: They were all illegitimate children of Charles II (of which there were twelve in total). The king had no legitimate heirs (Charles' wife, Catherine of Braganza, had three miscarriages), and it was his brother James II who eventually succeeded to the throne.

In 1685 **James Scott** (1649–85) led the Monmouth Rebellion, with the aim of deposing his uncle King James II. There was widespread opposition to the king's Catholic leanings, and the duke tried to harness this ill feeling, reminding everyone that he was a Protestant son of Charles II and declaring himself the rightful king. The rebellion failed, however, and he was beheaded for treason at the Tower of London on 15 July 1685. Ironically, James II was deposed in 1688.

Henry FitzRoy, meaning 'son of the king' (1663–90), supported James II during the Monmouth Rebellion. He was a loyal commander of royal troops in 1685, but ambitious men are notoriously fickle, and in 1688 he sided with the supporters of William of Orange, husband of James II's sister Mary. The king was defeated and deposed in that year. Henry died two years later, aged 27, after receiving a wound during King William III's wars in Ireland.

Charles FitzCharles (1657–80), his last name meaning 'son of Charles', spent most of his life in Spain and Morocco. Also known as Don Carlos, he was a colonel in the 2nd Tangier Regiment, or Earl of Plymouth's Regiment of Foot. His death, at the age of 23, came during an unsuccessful battle to free the town of Tangier (which was then in English hands) from the blockading efforts of Sultan Moulay Ismail of Morocco in 1680. His killer was dysentery.

Which of these men has not been considered for sainthood by the Pope?

King Henry VI • King Charles I •
Robert Grosseteste, Bishop of Lincoln

ANSWER: Charles I.

King Henry VI (1421–71) was a child king deposed by Edward IV in 1461, reinstated by Warwick the Kingmaker in 1470, and imprisoned and murdered after the Battle of Tewkesbury in 1471. When his corpse began to bleed after death, it was taken as a holy sign. Religious cults sprang up, and 150 miracles were attributed to the king's saintly intervention. However, pleas to the Pope by Henrys VII and VIII to have him canonised failed. When Henry VIII turned his back on Catholicism, the holy case for Henry VI was shelved forever.

King Charles I (1600–49) is the odd one out for two reasons: there was no *formal* attempt to canonise him (i.e. make him into a saint) – not that surprising, given that the English and Scottish thrones were officially Protestant; and five churches were actually dedicated to him ('Charles the Martyr'), making him the only non-saint to achieve this honour. His son Charles II made the date of his death, 30 January, a day of religious observance and penance.

Robert Grosseteste (1168–1253) was buried in Lincoln Cathedral, and almost immediately miracles were attributed to him. He had, however, fallen out with the Pope during his lifetime. He was a keen reformer of Church political abuses, which made him unpopular with Catholic HQ; and he once refused to accept a candidate named by the Pope for a position in the Diocese of Lincoln. There were several attempts to have him canonised, but on each occasion the miffed popes refused to listen.

These figures all had nicknames relating to metal. Who is the odd one out, and why?

Henry VIII • Oliver Cromwell • Margaret Thatcher

ANSWER: Henry VIII. His nickname referred to copper, while the other two had monikers featuring iron.

Henry VIII (1491–1547) was known as 'Old Coppernose' as a result of his cheap coinage – as spending ran wild in his court, and money began to run short, he began to cut down on the proportion of silver in his silver coins. Soon, only one third of each coin was made of silver – the remaining material in each coin was copper, resulting in a shiny red 'coppernose' as the silver rubbed away from the raised surface of the coin.

Oliver Cromwell (1599–1658) was known as 'Old Ironsides', after his old cavalry regiment, the Cambridgeshire Ironsides. The name was bestowed by King Charles I's nephew and cavalry commander, Prince Rupert. The Ironsides were the template for the New Model Army, founded by Cromwell in 1645. Ironically they did not have iron armour on their sides; only on the front, back and head.

British prime minister **Margaret Thatcher** (1925–2013) was known as 'the Iron Lady'. The nickname was given by a Soviet journalist in 1976, and was happily adopted by Thatcher. It came to symbolise her take-no-prisoners approach to politics. In 2007 she became the first living PM to have a statue unveiled at the House of Commons. At the ceremony she declared: 'I might have preferred iron – but bronze will do … It won't rust.'

What do these three men have in common?

?

Spencer Perceval •
Louis Mountbatten • Horatio Herbert Kitchener

LORD KITCHENER SAYS:-

'MEN, MATERIALS & MONEY ARE THE IMMEDIATE NECESSITIES. ......

DOES THE CALL OF DUTY FIND NO RESPONSE IN YOU UNTIL REINFORCED — LET US RATHER SAY SUPERSEDED — BY THE CALL OF COMPULSION?'

ENLIST TO-DAY.

ANSWER: All three were assassinated, although the exact circumstances of Kitchener's death have never been proven.

Spencer Perceval (1762–1812) became prime minister in 1809, and was assassinated in office on 11 May 1812. The assassin, John Bellingham, gunned him down in the House of Commons lobby. Perceval's last words are said to have been either 'Murder!' or 'Oh my god!'. Bellingham seems to have acted in a spirit of revenge rather than revolution. He had sought compensation for his imprisonment in Russia, but his pleas to the government had been rejected. He was hanged a week after the murder.

Louis Mountbatten, 1st Earl Mountbatten of Burma (1900–79), was born Prince Louis of Battenberg. In 1979 he was holidaying at his summer home in County Sligo, Ireland. Ignoring the worries of his security guards and the local police, he went fishing for lobsters and tuna. While the yacht was at sea, the Provisional Irish Republican Army (IRA) detonated the bomb they had planted in his yacht, killing Mountbatten and four others. He was actually taken from the water by fishermen while still alive, but died shortly afterwards.

Field Marshal Horatio Herbert Kitchener (1850–1916), 1st Earl Kitchener, is the iconic figure with the heavily moustachioed face glaring from First World War enlisting posters insisting that 'Your Country Needs You'. He was already a famous war veteran – 'Lord Kitchener of Khartoum' – when he became Secretary of State for War in 1914. He was killed on a diplomatic mission to Russia in 1916 when his ship, HMS *Hampshire*, struck a German mine near the Orkney Islands. Some said the sinking had been planned by the British Government, to get rid of a man who had become a liability; others said that the Russians had planned the assassination; many more said that the ship had been betrayed as an act of revenge by Captain Fritz Joubert Duquesne, one of Kitchener's enemies from the Boer War days in South Africa.

Only one of these royal pretenders avoided execution. Which?

Lambert Simnel • Perkin Warbeck •
John Deydras

ANSWER: Lambert Simnel.

Lambert Simnel (1477–c. 1535) was groomed for his role as king by Oxford priest Richard Simon. Originally he was going to be passed off as Richard, Duke of York, one of the murdered sons of King Edward IV, but after the hushed-up execution of the young Earl of Warwick, nephew of Edward, Simnel took on his identity, his supporters claiming that Warwick had escaped prison. Simnel was crowned King Edward VI on 24 May 1487, in preparation for a rebellion against Tudor king Henry VII. The ruse and uprising failed, but Henry took pity on Simnel and allowed him to work in the royal kitchens. He later became a royal falconer, and died around 1535.

Perkin Warbeck (c. 1477–99) was another pretender who challenged Henry VII earlier in his reign. He claimed to be Richard, Duke of York (Simnel's original pretend incarnation), son of King Edward IV, whose murder in the Tower of London was accompanied by rumours of escape and survival. Some have claimed that Warbeck was Edward IV's illegitimate son, or even the genuine Richard of York. None of those claims prevented him from being hanged at Tyburn in 1499, aged 22, however.

John Deydras (? –1318) turned up at the royal court in Oxford in 1318, claiming to be the real King Edward II. He said that as a toddler he had been swapped for a carter's son by a panicking nurse, after his ear had been chewed off by a pig. At Deydras' trial he claimed that the Devil, in the shape of his pet cat, had told him to do it. He was hanged, drawn and quartered in 1318, along with the poor cat.

Which one of these buildings is not a royal residence for Prince Charles?

Chevening House • Llwynywermod •
Delnadamph Lodge

ANSWER: Chevening House.

Chevening House is near Sevenoaks in Kent. Prince Charles was pencilled in as resident in 1974, at a time when his likeliest wife-to-be seemed to be Amanda Knatchbull, granddaughter of Lord Mountbatten. In 1980 he formally renounced his residency (even though he had never lived there), opting to purchase Highgrove House in Gloucestershire instead. Since then Chevening has been an official residence of the UK Foreign Secretary.

Llwynywermod is owned by Prince Charles; or, to be more precise, the Duchy of Cornwall. It is a 192-acre estate near Myddfai in Carmarthenshire, part of the Brecon Beacons National Park. It is the most recent royal residence, purchased in March 2007. It is where Charles and Camilla go when they are slumming it, being a modest three-bedroom farmhouse.

Delnadamph Lodge is part of the Balmoral estate, and was handed to Charles and Diana, Princess of Wales by Queen Elizabeth II as a wedding present. Diana did not like it, however, and renovations only began in earnest in 2007. It is another country retreat for Charles and Camilla (a bit more spacious than Llwynywermod, with twelve bedrooms). It is a mere 12 miles from another of Charles' pads, Birkhall, which he inherited from Queen Elizabeth, the Queen Mother.

Which of these people did not have a tattoo?

King Edward VII • Lady Randolph Churchill •
Lord Horatio Nelson

ANSWER: Lord Horatio Nelson.

King Edward VII (1841–1910) got the first of his many tattoos, a Maltese Cross, in 1862 while he was still the Prince of Wales. It was put on his arm by tattooist François Souwan during a visit to Jerusalem. Edward's sons, the Duke of Clarence and the Duke of York (later George V), were also tattooed. George had several pieces of body art including a dragon, tattooed in 1882 during a trip to Japan.

Lady Randolph Churchill (1854–1921), mother of Winston, had a snake tattooed on her right wrist. In the late nineteenth century it was briefly fashionable for aristocrats to have tattoos, possibly following the Prince of Wales' trend-setting. Lady Churchill was said to conceal the snake with a bracelet on formal occasions.

Lord Horatio Nelson (1758–1805), in spite of a career in the Navy, a calling long associated with tattoos, left his skin unstained. He was keen on compromising the skin of other creatures, however. During an expedition to the North Pole as a young man, his ship was temporarily trapped by ice. To pass the time, Nelson took his gun and chased a passing polar bear. He was ordered back on deck, and when asked why he had risked his life in such a manner he replied, 'I wished, Sir, to get the skin for my father.' Sadly, the story may be apocryphal.

All three were hanged — but only one died. Which one?

William Duell • John Lee • Robert Goodale

ANSWER: Robert Goodale.

William Duell was a 16 year old convicted of rape and murder at Acton in London. He was hanged at Tyburn on 24 November 1740, and left dangling for twenty minutes. His body was then cut down and taken for dissection. He was lying on the slab when someone noticed that he was breathing. Two hours later he was sitting up, with no memory of the hanging at all. He was returned to Newgate Prison, and his sentence was changed to transportation to the penal colony in Virginia for life.

John Lee was accused of murder at Babbacombe in Devon in 1884, and sent for execution at Exeter Gaol. Three times the executioner pulled the lever that was supposed to open the trapdoor that sent victims to their deaths, but nothing happened. Whenever anyone else stood on the trapdoor and held on to the rope, it worked. After the third failure, Lee was sent back to prison, where he remained into old age. The sorry saga was the theme of Fairport Convention's 1971 concept album 'Babbacombe Lee'.

Robert Goodale wasn't so lucky. He was a farmer, condemned for murdering his wife at Walsoken in Norfolk. He was hanged by executioner James Berry in 1885 (the man who had attempted to dispatch John Lee) at Norwich Castle. Due to a miscalculation, Berry made the rope too short, and Goodale's head was torn off in the plummet.

These Christian saints were once venerated in England, but only one of them was human. Which one?

St Michael • St Aldate • St Amphibalus

ANSWER: St Aldate.

St Michael is an archangel, responsible for casting Lucifer from Heaven. He is God's Commander-in-Chief, and is said to be so powerful that he can rescue souls from Hell – well worth directing a few prayers towards, and helping to explain his huge popularity. He is often depicted defeating a dragon (i.e. the Devil), an image partly hijacked by St George.

St Aldate was once thought to be a mutated form of 'Old Gate', based – it is thought – on the street St Aldate's, a thoroughfare in Oxford. Historians now believe that he did actually exist, however, under the name Eldad. He was probably a British bishop killed by pagan Saxons in the sixth century; but little more can be speculated.

According to legend, **St Amphibalus** was a British priest rescued from soldiers by St Alban in the third century. Alban, a pagan at the time, sheltered Amphibalus and wore his cloak to act as a decoy so that the priest could escape. Later historians examined the source texts and realised that the word 'Amphibalus' referred to the cloak itself, not a man. This failed to discourage the cult, however: Amphibalus was said to have converted thousands of Britons to Christianity, and in the twelfth century the priest's bones were discovered in St Albans. All very cloak and dagger.

Which of these extinct animals has not been sighted in modern Britain?

Plesiosaur • Pterodactyl • Icthyosaur

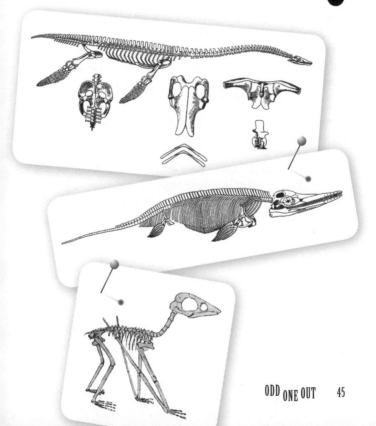

ANSWER: Icthyosaur.

The Loch Ness Monster is said by some to be a **plesiosaur** (possibly an elasmosaurus). The theory's biggest advocate was Sir Peter Scott, founder of the World Wildlife Fund. He painted pictures of the supposed beast, and even gave it a Latin name, *Nessiteras rhombopteryx* – 'the Ness creature with the diamond-shaped fin' (a name inspired by alleged snaps of the beast's fin, taken by underwater camera in the 1970s). Anagram fans soon noticed that Scott's Latin moniker could be rearranged to say 'Monster hoax by Sir Peter S'.

A spate of **pterodactyl** sightings occurred in the 1980s, all in Yorkshire. The reptile was estimated to have a wingspan of 1.5 metres, and was very noisy, either grunting like a pig or screaming like a herring gull. Observers mentioned the beast's huge leathery wings and laborious flight. It was widely reported in local newspapers, so it must be true.

The **icthyosaur** is one of the most British of all prehistoric reptiles, but it has never been spotted in modern times. The first specimen was liberated from Jurassic rocks at Lyme Regis in 1811 by proto-fossil hunter Mary Anning, and is still on display in the Natural History Museum, London. Dozens more have been found since, some with fossilised skin attached, and some with embryos inside.

What links these three twentieth-century servicemen?

Pilot Officer John C. Freeman •
Private John Parr • Pilot Officer John Noel Isaac

ANSWER: They all feature in 'first casualty of the war' records. Parr and Isaac were the first British men to die in their respective war arenas, whereas Freeman was the first man to kill someone in his.

RAF fighter pilot **John C. Freeman**, aged 19, and fellow pilot Paddy Byrne took off from Hornchurch in their Spitfires on 6 September 1939. They spotted two planes, machine-gunned them from the sky and returned in triumph, only to find themselves arrested. The planes they had shot down were British Hurricanes. The man shot by Byrne survived the ordeal, but Freeman's victim, Pilot Officer Montague Hulton-Harrop, was dead – the first RAF casualty of the war.

Private John Parr was shot dead on 21 August 1914. Aged 16 (he had lied about his age in order to enlist), he was a reconnaissance cyclist for the 4th Middlesex Regiment, scouting the roads on the French-Belgian border to look for the enemy. Sadly, they were soon located, near the village of Odbourg in Belgium, and Parr was killed. He is buried in St Symphorien military cemetery near Mons, and was the first British soldier killed in the First World War. On the gravestone his age is given as 20, a monument to the success of the lie that had got him shot in the first place. By spooky coincidence, his grave faces that of George Edwin Ellison, the last British soldier killed in the war.

Just one hour and fifty minutes after Britain's declaration of war on 3 September 1939, 28 year-old **Pilot Officer John Noel Isaac** of 600 Squadron crashed his Bristol Blenheim fighter-bomber. He was the first man to die in the war, before the conflict had even had a chance to start. Three days later the second casualty occurred when Pilot Officer Hulton-Harrop was gunned down by friendly fire (see above).

Which of these names for early police forces is the odd one out?

Mr Fielding's Men • Bobbies • Peelers

ANSWER: Mr Fielding's Men. They are the only ones not named after Robert Peel.

Mr Fielding's Men were better known as the Bow Street Runners, but had the much duller official title 'Principal Officers'. They were a pre-Metropolitan Police law and order force mobilised by Henry (1707–54) and John Fielding (1721–80) in 1749 (the former being the author of the novel *The History of Tom Jones, a Foundling*). The idea was that a 'Runner' would be available twenty-four hours a day, to travel to the scene of the crime and collar the culprit. The men were paid a retainer, and also earned money from rewards gathered from grateful victims and the State, upon conviction. The original Fielding's Men numbered just six.

Sir Robert Peel (1788–1850) served as prime minister on two separate occasions, reformed the country's judicial system in 1827, established the Metropolitan Police in 1829, and set the seeds for the Conservative Party (built from the ashes of the Tory Party) in 1834. His followers went on to form the Liberal Party in 1859. It was in 1822, as Home Secretary, that he invented the modern concept of a police force. The officers were named **'Bobbies'** or **'Peelers'** after him. By 1857 all cities in the UK had a police force, based on 'Peelian Principles'.

Which one of these structures can you still see in the UK?

?

Belle Tout Lighthouse •
Old London Bridge • Agecroft Hall

ANSWER: All three were relocated from their original sites, but Belle Tout Lighthouse is the only one that stayed in the UK.

Belle Tout was built in 1831 on the East Sussex coast. Following a century and a half of gradual cliff erosion, it was relocated more than 17 metres (50ft) inland in 1999. The 850-tonne granite building was not dismantled, but lifted from its foundations and pushed by hydraulic jacks along four steel and concrete beams. The new site has been designed to make future erosion-inspired relocations easier.

In 1968 **Old London Bridge** was purchased by Robert P. McCulloch of McCulloch Oil. Rumour has it that McCulloch thought he was buying the iconic Tower Bridge rather than the utilitarian London Bridge built by John Rennie in 1831. He shipped his prize to Lake Havasu City, Arizona. Spanning a canal and surrounded by an English theme park, mock-Tudor shopping mall and all, it was opened to the public in 1971. To make it even more of a botched job, bits of the bridge were left in England in lieu of tax duties. Arizona's folly is therefore a concrete frame, clad with stones from Rennie's London Bridge.

Agecroft Hall, built in the late fifteenth century, used to decorate the banks of the River Irwell in Pendlebury, Lancashire (Greater Manchester). In 1925 Thomas C. Williams Jr bought it, dismantled it and shipped it to Richmond, Virginia, where it now stands as the jewel in the crown of a mock-Tudor estate on the banks of the James River.

Which of these famous corpses did not have its equally famous head put on public display?

Oliver Cromwell • Jeremy Bentham • King Charles I

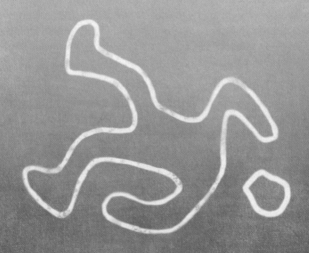

ANSWER: King Charles I.

The body of **Oliver Cromwell** (1599–1658) was embalmed, but the job was botched. The bits were buried in Westminster Abbey with minimal fuss but, in 1661, vengeful Royalists dug him up and hanged him at Tyburn. The head was put on a spike at Westminster Hall, and was still there when diarist Samuel Pepys paid a visit in the 1680s. In 1960 the head was laid to rest in the antechapel of Sidney Sussex College, Cambridge, where Cromwell had studied as an undergraduate between 1616 and 1617.

Jeremy Bentham (1748–1832) was the country's leading philosopher and social reformer. He donated his body to science, and asked for his remains to be displayed after death as an 'auto-icon'. The skeleton still sits in a cabinet at University College London, padded with straw, dressed in Bentham's clothes and topped with an effigy head (due to the poorly mummified one looking too macabre). The real head used to lie between the auto-icon's feet, but was so regularly kidnapped by college jokers that it was put into storage.

King Charles I (1600–49) is one of history's most famous decapitees, but his head was never on public display. When the king's coffin was examined in the mid-nineteenth century, it was reported that the head was well preserved, with some of the flesh, one eye and most of the hair, including a short pointed beard, intact. In that case, he is also the odd one out on account of accidental mummification.

Three famous ancient stately homes — but which is the only one still standing?

Clumber Park • High Head Castle • Costessey Hall

ANSWER: High Head Castle, albeit in a ruined state.

Clumber Park in Nottinghamshire was built in the 1760s for the Duke of Newcastle. Fires in 1879 and 1912 destroyed much of the house. In the first fire the central section of the building was gutted, and by the time of the second fire the owner, the 7th Duke of Newcastle, had moved out. The house was finally demolished in 1938. The remaining park and lake is now a popular National Trust property.

The surviving shell of **High Head Castle** near Ivegill in Cumbria dates from the mid-eighteenth century. Perched on a crag 100ft above the River Ive, it is still impressive. Decaying through the decades, in 1956 fire gutted the entire building, leaving just the walls. In 1985 an application was made to demolish the picturesque fragment; but it managed to survive. Plans are perpetually afoot to renovate.

Costessey Hall near Norwich was built in the 1550s by Sir Henry Jernegan, after Queen Mary I gave him the Manor of Costessey as a reward for his support in her claim to the throne. This original building was incorporated into a huge Gothic folly in the 1830s. With the death of the last owner in 1913, the building was requisitioned by the War Office. Soldiers stationed here literally wrecked the building, and it was pulled down after the end of the First World War in 1918.

Three historical figures, three famous lanterns — but which is the only one of these three lights not to survive?

King Alfred the Great • Guy Fawkes • Florence Nightingale

ANSWER: King Alfred's.

A time-keeping lantern was invented during the reign of **King Alfred the Great** (849–99). It consisted of a candle surrounded by translucent ox-horn. As sections of the candle burned down, monks were able to tell when it was time for prayers, lunch, and so on. The Ashmolean Museum in Oxford has in its collection a lantern originally described as Alfred's. It is now known to be of twelfth-century German origin.

Guy Fawkes' lantern – the one he was carrying when soldiers interrupted his attempts to blow up the Houses of Parliament – can be seen in the Ashmolean Museum in Oxford. Like Alfred's, the lamp had a window made of thin horn, with a door to close off all light during tricky moments in the course of terrorism. The relic was given to Oxford University in 1641 by Robert Heywood, the son of a Justice of the Peace present when Fawkes was caught on 5 November 1605.

Florence Nightingale was dubbed 'the lady with the lamp' on account of the lantern she carried during hospital work in the Crimean War (1854–56). The nickname was first coined in a poem by Henry Longfellow in 1858. The Florence Nightingale Museum has one of her Turkish candle lanterns on display. Like many lanterns of eastern origin, the body is made from paper – thick and crinkled like a concertina.

Which of these three bearded baddies is fictional?

Redbeard • Blackbeard • Bluebeard

ANSWER: Bluebeard.

Redbeard (Barbarossa in Italian) was the nickname of Baba Aruj, otherwise known as Baba Oruc (1474–1518), a Barbary pirate and governor of Algiers. All three of his siblings were pirates too and, to add to the confusion, one of them, Hayreddin Pasha, assumed the 'Barbarossa' nickname when Aruj died in battle against Spaniards in Algeria.

Blackbeard was also known as Edward Teach (1680–1718), an English pirate whose hunting grounds were the West Indies and American coast. He was schooled in piracy by Benjamin Hornigold, who first took Teach on board in 1716. The men formed a double act, carrying out many dastardly sea-dog deeds and managing to get four pirate ships in their fleet, one of them captained by the impressively named Stede Bonnet. When Hornigold hung up his wooden leg, eye patch and parrot for the last time in 1718, Blackbeard continued, undisputed terror of the high seas.

The grisly tale of **Bluebeard** was popularised by writer Charles Perrault in 1697. An ugly, blue-bearded nobleman, he has been piling up the bodies of his dead wives in his cellar. His latest wife discovers the crimes, and narrowly escapes the same fate herself. Bluebeard is possibly based on murderous French nobleman Gilles de Rais.

Three ringleaders of the 1381 Peasants' Revolt — but which one did not die during the uprising?

Wat Tyler • Jack Straw • John Ball

ANSWER: Jack Straw, who didn't actually exist.

Wat Tyler (1341–81) led the rebels in Kent, and parleyed with Richard II in London. The proceedings came to an end after Richard promised to carry out all the rebels' revolutionary, egalitarian demands, which seems to have caught them by surprise. The Mayor of London scuppered this nonsense by killing Tyler with his sword, after which the other ringleaders were rounded up and executed.

Jack Straw was mentioned by writer Geoffrey Chaucer in *The Canterbury Tales*, cementing his fame. He appears to have been invented either as a result of confusion with a nickname for Kent rebel leader Wat Tyler, or a mix-up with John Wrawe, a Suffolk priest who led rebels in that county. Undeterred, legend says Straw was executed in 1381 as one of the ringleaders.

John Ball (1338–81) was a priest who preached equality, coming up with the couplet 'When Adam delved and Eve span, Who was then the gentleman?' This implied that there was no divine command for the kind of repressive hierarchy under which the peasantry toiled. Ball was hunted down in Coventry and hanged, drawn and quartered in the presence of Richard II.

Which of these British traditions is the most infrequent?

Hunting the Mallard, Oxford
• Planting the Penny Hedge, Whitby •
Preston Guild, Preston

ANSWER: Hunting the Mallard – it happens once a century.

Hunting the Mallard takes place on 14 January at All Souls' College. It is said to have originated with a giant mallard discovered when the college was being built in the mid-fifteenth century, although records only go back to 1632. The ceremony consists of a college parade with burning torches and a duck (replaced with an effigy in the 2001 ceremony). Always a drunken affair, in 1701 the custom was limited to once a century. The next hunt is due in 2101.

Planting the Penny Hedge (or Horngarth) takes place every year. In 1159, three hunters pursuing a wild boar got overexcited and killed a religious hermit. As penance, they and their heirs had to build a hazel fence strong enough to withstand three tides on the east side of Whitby harbour.

Preston Guild has become proverbial – 'once in a Preston Guild' means something that happens very infrequently. The event was first held in 1179 to establish the 'Guild Merchant', a monopoly to which all town traders had to belong. The annual Guild was the time to renew membership, but in 1542 it was decided that once every twenty years was sufficient. In 1790 the town introduced freedom of trade; but the Guild was so popular that it continued, as a once-in-a-Preston-Guild town carnival. The next is due in 2032.

Which of these men was the first to be hanged, drawn and quartered in Britain?

Dafydd ap Gruffydd •
William Wallace • David Tyrie

ANSWER: That dubious honour fell to Dafydd ap Gruffudd.

Dafydd ap Gruffydd (1238–83) was the last prince of an independent Wales, and the first person to undergo the terminal ordeal, in 1238. The punishment was dreamt up by the ruthless King Edward I of England. The prince was captured during a battle at Hawarden Castle, part of the Welsh struggle to prevent English conquest. Accused of plotting the death of the king (high treason), he was also condemned for daring to start a war during Lent!

Scottish rebel leader **William Wallace** (? –1305) was another of Edward's victims. He was captured in 1305 at Robroyston, near Glasgow, seven years after his army's final defeat at the Battle of Falkirk in 1298. He was executed at Smithfield after a swift trial, in which he was accused of treason and the medieval equivalent of crimes against humanity. His very pertinent line of defence was: 'I could not be a traitor to Edward, for I was never his subject.'

David Tyrie (? –1782) was the last man to be hanged, drawn and quartered in Britain. Accused of spying for the French, he was condemned for treason and executed in front of a crowd 100,000 on Southsea Common. A reporter noted: 'There was only one thing which gave him concern, which was, that his father was living, and he feared this misfortune would bring his grey hairs with sorrow to the grave. He declined saying a word to the populace, observing that he knew not why he was to feed or gratify the idle curiosity of the multitude. He never hung his head the whole time.'

Which of these drinks was the first to be sold in shops in Britain?

Tea • Coffee • Chocolate

ANSWER: All three became fashionable in the 1650s, and no one knows with certainty which came first, although coffee seems the likeliest.

Tea was introduced into Europe from China in the 1600s, but was not advertised in the English press until 1658. Catherine of Braganza, new wife of Charles II, was its first champion. She sailed into Portsmouth on 13 May 1662, and her first request on landfall was for a cup of tea. There was none to be had, and Catherine was offered a glass of ale instead. She, like many a queen since, was not amused. From 1662 onwards, tea became a fashionable drink.

Coffee arrived in Europe in 1615, and in May 1637 Greek student Nathaniel Conopios brewed Britain's first cup of coffee, at Balliol College in Oxford. Fourteen years later, Oxford opened the country's first coffee house. By 1700 there were 3,000 coffee houses in London alone.

Spanish Conquistador Don Hernán Cortés introduced South American cocoa beans to Spain in 1528. **Chocolate** became a popular drink there, and across much of Europe, although it only gained a foothold in Britain in the 1650s. It was very much a luxury beverage, and madly expensive.

All three of these men were sons of King George III. Which one was Queen Victoria's father?

King George IV (died 1830)
• King William IV (died 1837) •
Prince Edward, the Duke of Kent (died 1820)

ANSWER: Prince Edward.

It was an unlikely succession, as Victoria was only fifth in line to the throne at birth. In front of her in the royal queue were her three uncles: the Prince Regent (later **George IV**); Prince Frederick, the Duke of York; the Duke of Clarence (later **William IV**), and her father, **Prince Edward**. It was possible that cousins or male siblings might appear at some point too, which would shunt her even further down the line. However, George IV and Prince Frederick were both separated from their wives (both of whom were past child-bearing age); William IV's two daughters died in infancy; George III and Victoria's father both died in 1820; and Prince Frederick died in 1827. George IV bowed out in 1830, and Victoria was suddenly next in line after her uncle, William IV. She was the last of the House of Hanover: her son Edward VII was 'of Saxe-Coburg and Gotha', the dukedom of his father Prince Albert. The house name was hastily changed to 'Windsor' in 1917, as it sounded embarrassingly German for a country suddenly at war with Germany.

Which of these Scottish sites contains the oldest extant building in Britain?

Skara Brae • Broch of Mousa • Knap of Howar

ANSWER: Knap of Howar.

Skara Brae is an entire Neolithic settlement, at the Bay of Skaill on Mainland, Orkney. The eight houses here were in use between 1200 and 500 BC. As Europe's best-preserved ancient village, it gained UNESCO World Heritage Site status in 1999.

The **Broch of Mousa** on Shetland is the oldest broch (round tower) in Scotland, and the best-preserved too. It is a relative youngster on this page, however, built around 100 BC.

The Neolithic farmstead at **Knap of Howar** on Papa Westray, Orkney, dates back to 3700 BC, and may be the oldest house in northern Europe still standing. Occupied for around 900 years, the house has two sections, each containing a sea-facing door – the original 'room with a view'.

Which of these ancient monuments was constructed most recently?

Wayland's Smithy •
Stonehenge • Avebury stone circles

ANSWER: Stonehenge – although it is the most iconic of ancient monuments, it is the youngest of the three.

Wayland's Smithy near Ashbury in Oxfordshire was constructed around 3700 BC, with an extension added 300 years later. It is a Neolithic burial mound, later associated with the Saxon god of ironworking, Wayland (also known as Weland or Wolund, the Germanic version of the Roman god Vulcan).

The construction of **Stonehenge** began in 2600 BC. Various theories have declared it the work of the magician Merlin, a group of petrified giants, a cattle corral, and a religious temple. The word 'henge' has its origin with this site, meaning 'hanging' (i.e. stones suspended in the air by other stones).

Avebury's stone structures, bank and ditch were erected/constructed between 2850 and 2200 BC. The outer stones enclose 11.5 hectares, including most of Avebury village (with the notable exception of the church). The preservation and modern form of the site is largely down to marmalade heir Alexander Keiller, who re-erected some of the stones and marked out the site of missing ones in the 1930s – all detailed in Avebury Museum.

Which of these societies was established most recently?

The Royal Society for the Prevention of Cruelty to Animals (RSPCA) • The National Society for the Prevention of Cruelty to Children (NSPCC) • The Society for Effecting the Abolition of the Slave Trade

ANSWER: The NSPCC. Anti-slavery came first, but animal protection beat child protection by a surprising sixty years.

The **SPCA** was founded in 1824 (the 'R' came after the coronation of the society's patron, Princess Victoria). There were twenty-two founders, including William Wilberforce and the most influential animal rights campaigner of the time, Richard 'Humanity Dick' Martin, MP for Galway. The twenty-two first met in Old Slaughter's Coffee House in London – an appropriate or inappropriate name, depending on how you look at it.

In 1881, Reverend George Staite wrote to the *Liverpool Mercury*: '...whilst we have a Society for the Prevention of Cruelty to Animals, can we not do something to prevent cruelty to children?' Social reformers of the time, such as Lord Shaftesbury, countered: 'The evils you state are enormous and indisputable, but they are of so private, internal and domestic a nature as to be beyond the reach of legislation.' Regardless, on 8 July 1884, the London Society for the Prevention of Cruelty to Children, later to become the **NSPCC**, was founded.

The **Society for Effecting the Abolition of the Slave Trade** formed on 22 May 1787, four years after the first anti-slavery petition was handed to Parliament. There were twelve founders, including nine Quakers – prime movers since German and Dutch-born Quakers in Pennsylvania signed a declaration against slavery in 1688.

Which PM was the oldest on his last day in office?

William Gladstone
• Winston Churchill •
Harold Macmillan

ANSWER: William Gladstone.

William Gladstone (1809–98) was 88 on his last day in office on 2 March 1898. The third of his four terms had ushered in the Representation of the People Act 1884, extending suffrage in the UK. You were now eligible to vote if you were a male who owned land worth at least £10, or paid an annual rental of at least £10 (approximately £600 in today's money). This reform brought the total British electorate to over 5.5 million – roughly 60 per cent of the male population.

Winston Churchill (1874–1965) was 81 when he retired on 7 April 1955. His last stint in power, 1951–55, was overshadowed by ill health. He had suffered a mild stroke two years previously, with a more severe attack in June 1953. After his return to the political stage at the Conservative party conference in October, it was clear to all that his physical and mental powers had been dealt a severe blow. He stepped down as prime minister in 1955.

Harold Macmillan (1894–1986) was a mere 69 when he left office on 18 October 1963. After retiring from frontline politics he filled his time by writing a gigantic six-volume autobiography for his family publishing business, Macmillan. He also served as Chancellor of Oxford University from 1960 until his death in 1986. He never shied away from political or intellectual confrontation and famously criticised the Thatcher government for demonising miners – 'the best men in the world, who beat the Kaiser's and Hitler's armies and never gave in' – during the miners' strike between 1984 and 1985.

Pitt the Younger, at 24, is far and away the youngest PM to take office. Who is the second youngest?

Augustus FitzRoy • Robert Peel • Tony Blair

ANSWER: Augustus FitzRoy.

Augustus FitzRoy (1735–1811), Duke of Grafton and leader of the Whig party, was just 33 when he took office in 1768. He was criticised during his premiership for not taking a firmer hand against the French. Britain had emerged from the Seven Years' War (1756–63) as the world's pre-eminent colonial power, and FitzRoy's critics accused him of weakness in allowing the French to annex Corsica in 1769.

Robert Peel (1788–1850) was 46 when he became PM in 1834, and he left his policeman's boot-sized print on the affairs of the nation. He was the founder of the proto-police force known in England as Bobbies and in Ireland as Peelers, as well as a key figure in forging the modern Conservative party from the ashes of the Tory party, via the Tamworth Manifesto of 1834.

Tony Blair (1953–) was 43 in 1997 when New Labour toppled the Tories, becoming the first Labour PM in eighteen years. He set out with the intention of modernising Government meetings, insisting on being called 'Tony', doing away with ties and, as related elsewhere in this book, banning moustaches. The new influx of female ministers found those last two easy to comply with.

Which of these Scottish loch monsters is said to be an omen of death?

The Loch Ness Monster •
Morag of Loch Morar • Lizzie of Loch Lochy

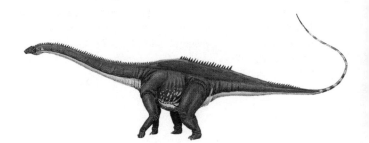

ANSWER: Morag of Loch Morar.

The **Loch Ness Monster** is the most famous of her breed, and was last spotted in 2011.

Originally, **Morag of Loch Morar**, the deepest freshwater lake in the British Isles, was a cross between a mermaid and a banshee (the spirit that haunts and screeches before a notable death). In British folklore, sighting either of these creatures is an omen of death. Morag used to weep and wail when local landowners were about to die, and was last verified as doing so in 1898. In the twentieth century, however, she became confused with Nessie, and was described as a serpent-like monster. She was spotted for the last time in 1969, when two gun-toting fishermen in a boat encountered her and one of them opened fire. Morag sank beneath the water, and has not been spied since.

Loch Lochy is home to **Lizzie** (one of three Scottish lochs containing a creature of that name). She was spotted regularly during the twentieth century, and from descriptions she appears to be whale-like, somewhere between 6 and 10 metres long. She was last spotted in 1997.

Which of these is the only one, according to folklore, not to have visited the British Isles?

St Peter • Jesus • The Virgin Mary

ANSWER: St Peter.

There is no historical tradition of **St Peter** visiting Britain, although Christian lore casts him as the founder of all the Christian nations of Europe. At various points throughout history this has been taken literally, and it has been suggested that he did indeed come here to get the first church up and running. The chapel of the Venerable English College in Rome shows Peter in a fresco doing just this.

Jesus was said to have visited as a child, with his uncle Joseph of Arimathea. This was not Joseph the husband of Mary, but the man who took charge of Jesus' body after the crucifixion, having donated his own tomb-in-waiting to the cause. In legend he came with Jesus to Cornwall to kick-start the tin-mining industry, and in later life returned to spread Christianity, notably at Glastonbury, where a thorn tree said to be descended from his staff still flowers every Christmas.

According to legend, **the Virgin Mary** paid a visit after the death of Jesus, during the first wave of Christian persecutions. She travelled from Palestine to the embryonic Christian community set up by Joseph of Arimathea in Britain. Legend places her in the Hebrides, chiefly Iona. Mary Magdalene apparently took a long Scottish holiday hereabouts too.

The fact underlying these legends is that early churches were able to harvest prestige, pilgrims and (most importantly) cash if they could prove a link with the heroes of the Bible.

Three men have been put forward as the real author of Shakespeare's plays — but only two have surviving works. Who is the odd one out?

Edward de Vere, 17th Earl of Oxford • William Stanley, 6th Earl of Derby • Christopher Marlowe

ANSWER: William Stanley.

Proponents of **Edward de Vere**, 17th Earl of Oxford (1550–1604), also have a strong case. The known facts of the man's life tie in compellingly with themes in the Bard's plays. The argument is that a courtier could not officially be a playwright, and so willing stooge and struggling actor W. Shakespeare, esq. of Stratford upon Avon was roped in. The theory is undermined, however, by the known poetic outpourings of de Vere, which are pretty dismal.

William Stanley, 6th Earl of Derby (1561–1642) is a strong contender for the quill of the Bard, with details in his life finding uncanny echoes in the plays. The theory is either undermined or bolstered, depending on how you look at it, by the fact that no literary work of Stanley has survived. Oliver Cromwell's soldiers burnt down his family seat at Lathom House, Lancashire, in 1642 during the Civil War, which may explain posterity's loss.

It would be great if **Christopher Marlowe** (1564–93) had risen from his own ashes as Shakespeare, continuing the trajectory of artistic genius left off in his final play *Edward II* (1592), but history seems pretty adamant that he was stabbed to death in a pub in Deptford. Marlowe's story is one of espionage, unconformity and romantic skulduggery, so the conspiracy theorists have a lot to play with.

What do these three English villages have in common?

Wharram Percy in Yorkshire •
Godwick in Norfolk • Hampton-on-Sea in Kent

ANSWER: They have all been abandoned – though Hampton-on-Sea was the only one not indirectly destroyed by sheep!

Wharram Percy in North Yorkshire was rediscovered in 1948. First settled in pre-Roman times, it was thriving throughout the Norman period, and declined as a direct result of sheep farming. The village was emptied in the early sixteenth century after the sheepish lord of the manor booted everyone out and knocked down the houses to create new pasture for his flocks. The broken church remains, and the site is now looked after by English Heritage.

Godwick in Norfolk was also a victim of sheep pasture. At first glance there appears to be a surviving flint and brick church tower. This is a folly, however, built from the rubble when the thirteenth-century church was knocked down after the abandonment of the village in the seventeenth century. This re-erected folly itself suffered semi-collapse in 1981.

Hampton-on-Sea in Herne Bay, Kent, was a fishing village destroyed by coastal erosion. Its rise and fall was swift. Prior to 1864 it was a scatter of fishermen's cottages, and it was only expanded after 1879 following investment by an oyster fishery company. It was finally abandoned in 1916, just five years before the last bits of the village disappeared under the waves. A section of pier, an inn and the ruins of the clearly not very effective coastal defences are all that remain.

Which of these wives of Henry VIII is the odd one out?

Anne Boleyn • Catherine Howard •
Anne of Cleves

ANSWER: Anne of Cleves – she was the only one not beheaded, and also the only one never officially proclaimed Queen Consort.

Anne Boleyn (1501–36) was the daughter of the Duke of Wiltshire, and one of the aristocratic ladies who worked for Henry's first queen, Catherine of Aragon. It was Henry's infatuation with her (and his quest for a legitimate male heir) that led to the English Reformation. The Pope had refused to grant him a divorce, and so Henry made himself head of a reformed Church, enabling him to annul his own marriage. No male heir appeared, however: the birth of the future Elizabeth I was followed by three miscarriages, and Henry had Anne executed on trumped-up charges of high treason.

Catherine Howard (1523–42) was beheaded for adultery at the age of 19. On the night before her execution she had the beheading block brought into her room, so that she could practice how to position her head to ensure a clean blow from the sword. Her grim rehearsals paid off, and her head was removed with a single sword stroke (as was Anne Boleyn's).

Henry met **Anne of Cleves** (1515–57) for the first time shortly before their marriage. He declared her 'The Mare of Flanders' and, although they married, she never actually became Queen Consort. Henry gave Anne land and palaces after their divorce (including Anne Boleyn's family seat at Hever Castle), and her official title became 'The King's Beloved Sister'. She and Henry were good friends, and Anne outlived all the other wives, being present at the coronation of Mary I in 1553.

Who was above William the Conqueror in the medieval feudal hierarchy?

The Duke of Normandy •
The King of France • The Pope

ANSWER: The King of France.

After his conquest of the island in 1066, William was jointly King of England and Duke of Normandy. The dukes were descended (like the later English kings) from Vikings ('Norman' means 'North Man', i.e. Norse/Scandinavian). In the feudal system, the **Duke of Normandy** was a vassal of the French throne. This is the root of the centuries-long power struggle between the thrones of England and France. Feudalism was based on land ownership – the person at the top owned everything, and the ones beneath (even the Kings of England) were merely tenants.

The Popes were not part of the feudal system, but all western Christian kings were ruled by them in Church and spiritual matters.

Churchill fought in the Second Boer War in South Africa. What rank did he hold when he first arrived on the battlefield?

?

Private • Lieutenant •
None – he was there as a journalist

ANSWER: None – Churchill was war correspondent for the *Morning Post* newspaper. He became a lieutenant later in the war.

The Second Boer War began in October 1899, a conflict involving Britain and the South African Boer Republics. Churchill became a prisoner of war after the armoured train on which he was travelling was ambushed. His heroics before capture should have earned him the Victoria Cross, it was said, but this honour was only open to military men, and Churchill was a journalist at the time.

His escape from prison, and the subsequent 480km dash to the safe haven of Portuguese Lourenço Marques in Delagoa Bay were journalistic gold dust. He refused to return home with his diary of adventures for the *Morning Post*, however, joining the British Army at the Siege of Ladysmith and the taking of the town of Pretoria. He even managed to persuade General Redvers Buller, Commander-in-Chief of the British Army, to enlist him as lieutenant of the newly formed cavalry division, the South African Light Horse. One of the first men into the conquered Pretoria, fifty-two Boer prison camp guards surrendered to him and his cousin Charles Richard John Spencer-Churchill, 9th Duke of Marlborough.

Which of the following has not been put forward by historians as the cause of King George III's mental illness?

The genetically inherited disease porphyria •
Arsenic poisoning • Grief and stress resulting from
the death of his daughter Princess Amelia

ANSWER: Grief and stress.

The most commonly accepted theory is that George had inherited the disease **porphyria**, although some have argued that the king was poisoned by **arsenic**, possibly present in medicines, paints or cosmetics. George himself maintained that his disturbed mind was the result of stress induced by **grief** at the death of his daughter. Doctors of the time claimed that the king's blood contained 'evil humours' which only blood-letting and restraints would cure.

George's famous madness first bloomed in 1765, with the major episode in 1788 leading to full dementia in 1811, and the reign of his son as Prince Regent.

Which of these men was dubbed 'the most efficient executioner in British history'?

Albert Pierrepoint •
'Hanging' Judge Jeffreys • Jack Ketch

ANSWER: Albert Pierrepoint.

Chief Executioner **Albert Pierrepoint** (1905–92) was pre-eminent in stringing up people during the war years, including William 'Lord Haw Haw' Joyce, Ruth Ellis (the last woman hanged in Britain) and Belsen Commandant Josef Kramer. When Pierrepoint retired in 1956, after at least 450 executions (there are no official statistics), the Home Office called him 'the most efficient executioner in British history'. To their dismay, he went on to write that capital punishment was not a deterrent.

Judge George Jeffreys (1645–89), 1st Baron Jeffreys of Wem, and Lord Chancellor, achieved notoriety during the 'Bloody Assizes' in Taunton, following the quashed rebellion of the Duke of Monmouth. At the Assizes, Jeffreys condemned 300 to death, and had 900 more transported to penal colonies. He, too, became a nursery bogie ('if you don't go to sleep, Judge Jeffreys will come for you!' – that kind of thing).

Jack Ketch (? –1686) was the most inefficient executioner in British history. He worked under Charles II and James II, dispatching such noteworthy celebrities as the rebellious William Russell and the Duke of Monmouth, who attempted to overthrow Charles II and James II respectively. His executions (usually beheadings with an axe) were often botched, and after Russell's slow and agonising death Ketch even wrote a letter of apology to the man's family. Monmouth paid him to make a better job of his own execution, but it still took Ketch five blows to remove the head. Jack Ketch became synonymous with the role of executioner, as a nursery demon, a pseudonym for the Devil, and even a nickname for death itself.

Which of these Saxon leaders was the first man to be called 'King of England'?

Egbert • Alfred • Aethelstan

ANSWER: Aethelstan. This is a bit of a trick question, as the others were also kings of all the English territory available at the time.

In 827, having forced the Kingdom of Mercia (the southern Midlands) to submit to him two years previously, King **Egbert** of Wessex (770–839) leaped the final hurdle by conquering the Kingdom of Northumbria. This made Egbert the first person to reign over a united England. He did not use the King of England title, however; although the *Anglo-Saxon Chronicles* call him *bretwalda*, or 'over-king'.

Alfred, King of the West Saxons (849–99), was dubbed King of the Anglo-Saxons late in his reign. He was the first person to rule over all the surviving Saxon kingdoms. Alfred spent the early years of his reign battling the Danes; and the treaty he signed with Danish King Guthrum in 880 gave him the smaller portion of the island, centred on the south and southern midlands. Most of England was still held by the Danes, and so Alfred was never called 'King of England'.

In 927 **Aethelstan** (895–939) conquered the Danish Kingdom of York (the former Saxon kingdom of Northumbria). He had ruled the Kingdom of Wessex beforehand, but between 927 and 939 he was officially called 'King of England'. After his death the Danes returned and reconquered their ancestral bits of the island, and the Kingdom of York was not regained until 954.

Which of these sports has the earliest historical mention?

Golf • Cricket • Baseball

GOLF CALENDAR
By Edward Penfield
Published by R.H. Russell
1899

ANSWER: Golf – probably! Coincidentally, they all share 1744 as a key date.

Golf was first mentioned in 1261 in the Netherlands (*kolf*). China was knocking small balls into holes as early as the tenth century. Modern golf was developed in Scotland in the mid-1700s, although versions of 'gowf' had been played in Scotland for 300 years prior to this. Modern 18-hole golf is Scottish, and the oldest surviving golf rule book dates from 1744, printed in Edinburgh.

'Cricket' is also a Dutch word, based on *krick*, meaning a stick (same root as our word 'crutch', or the 'cruck' in a cruck barn). The first mention of *creckett* dates from 1598, in a court case referring to a game played by children fifty years earlier. The adult version is first mentioned in Sussex in 1611. Eleven-a-side games were established by the late seventeenth century. The Laws of Cricket were codified in 1744 and tidied up thirty years later. The MCC, founded at Lord's in 1787, was, from the outset, the keeper of the Laws of Cricket.

Baseball was first mentioned in 1744, in *A Little Pretty Pocket-Book*, by John Newbery, published in London. It developed from medieval English games such as rounders, stool-ball and tut-ball. The first recorded game was in 1749 in Surrey, featuring the Prince of Wales. American versions of the game varied in rules, and had additional names including town-ball and round-ball. The first codification of recognisably modern rules of play was in 1845 in New York.

Which of these ancient towns was not founded by the Romans?

Colchester, Essex • Reculver, Kent • Totnes, Devon

ANSWER: Totnes.

The town of Camulodunum, later known as **Colchester**, was already an ancient settlement when the Romans established a military fort here in AD 43. It became a colonia in AD 50, a place where decommissioned soldiers lived the good life. Its new name was Colonia Claudia Victricensis ('city of the victorious Claudius'). The town's surviving Roman walls and castle date from after AD 60, the year in which local British queen Boudicca burnt the town to the ground.

Reculver in Kent may have been the Romans' first staging post after they landed in Britain under Aulus Plautus in AD 43. Settlement here was limited to a coastal fort, probably hastily erected in the year of invasion. The proper fort, Regulbium, was founded in the second century.

In folklore, **Totnes** was the first town founded in Britain – not by the Romans, but by their legendary cousins, the Trojans. Brutus, great-great-grandson of King Priam of Troy, landed here in the twelfth century BC. However, in the real world, Totnes is a Saxon town first mentioned in AD 907, when it was fortified by King Edward the Elder as one of a number of walled towns in Devon.

Three nursery rhyme characters — but which one is not based on a real person?

Georgie Porgie • Humpty Dumpty • Dick Whittington

ANSWER: Humpty Dumpty.

Georgie Porgie is said to refer to King George IV (1762–1830). The rhyme suggests someone fat ('pudding and pie'), lecherous ('kissed the girls and made them cry') and cowardly ('Georgie Porgie ran away'), all in keeping with George's public persona. When he died, *The Times* obituary declared: 'If he ever had a friend, a devoted friend from any rank of life, we protest that the name of him or her never reached us'. However, the rhyme may not be about George at all – it may refer to Charles II, or royal favourite and all-round rakish type George Villiers, 1st Duke of Buckingham.

Humpty Dumpty (according to one theory) was a Royalist cannon placed on the wall of St Mary-at-the-Walls church in Colchester during the English Civil War. A Parliamentary cannon blasted a hole in the wall, causing Humpty to topple. The Royalists – 'all the King's horses and all the King's men' – tried to reposition it, without success. The name Humpty Dumpty predates this, dating to the fifteenth century as a derogatory reference to a fat person. The notion of Humpty as an egg was immortalised by Lewis Carroll and his illustrator Charles Tenniel in *Through the Looking Glass, and What Alice Found There* (1871).

Richard 'Dick' Whittington (1354–1423) was Lord Mayor of London four times, as well as a sheriff and MP. He made his fortune as a merchant, and may or may not have owned a cat (an essential feature of the legend). The 'cat' was possibly a type of ship (a cat, catch or ketch), with which he made his money. In a seventeenth-century engraving of Whittington, the original image had the man's hand resting on a skull. This was changed to a cat to mirror the irresistible legend.

In which one of these Shakespeare plays does Sir John Falstaff not appear?

Henry IV Part I • Henry IV Part II • Henry V

ANSWER: Henry V.

Although the plot of **Henry V** follows seamlessly from **Henry IV**, Falstaff is killed off in the first act, without actually appearing on stage.

In the two parts of Henry IV, the Falstaff character was originally called Sir John Oldcastle. The historical Oldcastle was a fifteenth-century religious rebel, one of the 'Lollards' who called for reformation of the established Church. He was burned for heresy and treason in 1417. The descendants of Sir John Oldcastle objected to the use of the name for the comic creation later known as Falstaff, and 'Oldcastle' was hastily dropped.

Incidentally, the three Henry VI plays, although portraying events after the death of Henry V, were written earlier than the other plays. One of the minor characters in the action is Sir John Fastolf – the origin of the name Sir John Falstaff. Fastolf had a reputation for greed and cowardice, and in Henry IV the character abandons the battlefield. He had no living descendants in Shakespeare's time, so his was a safe name to use.

Which of these writers is the odd one out?

Ellis Bell • George Eliot • Branwell Brontë

ANSWER: George Eliot – the other two are Brontës. (Branwell Brontë is also an acceptable answer, as he is the only male of the three writers.)

Ellis Bell (1818–48) was the early pen name of Emily Brontë, and she is the only one who had books published under two different names. Her first poems appeared under the pseudonym 'Ellis Bell', in the publication *Poems* (1840), a collaborative effort with her sisters Charlotte ('Currer Bell') and Anne ('Acton Bell'). *Wuthering Heights*, her only novel, had her real name on the cover.

George Eliot (1819–80), in addition to being the only one who wasn't a Brontë, is the only one whose entire output appeared under a pen name. The writer's real name was Mary Ann Evans, and her choice of pseudonym may have been inspired by the name of her lover, George Henry Lewes. The two lived together, unmarried, for twenty-five years – very scandalous at the time, and another reason why the author avoided using 'Mary Ann Evans'. Her books would have been attacked by the moral police of the day, regardless of content.

Branwell Brontë (1817–48) was the only one who did not achieve literary success in his lifetime. It is safe to say that his poems and stories are only known today through the fame of his three sisters: Charlotte, Emily and Anne Brontë.

What means of travel links these three men?

King Bladud • James Tytler • Samuel Franklin Cody

THE TIDAL WAVE

JULY 4.

95 Ships Launched

UNITED STATES SHIPPING BOARD EMERGENCY FLEET CORPORATION

ANSWER: All three were the first men to achieve certain forms of flight in Britain. (Bladud, being mythical, is the odd one out.)

King Bladud, founder of the city of Bath, invented a flying machine sometime around 1000 BC, based on a simple set of wings. He took off from his palace in London and managed a few twists and turns before losing control and crashing into the Temple of Apollo (near modern Temple Tube station). There were no survivors. The black box from which this information was taken is twelfth-century pseudo-historian Geoffrey of Monmouth's *History of the Kings of Britain*. In this case Geoffrey seems to have been inspired by the Greek myth of Icarus, who flew too close to the sun on home-made feather-and-wax wings, melting the binding agent.

James Tytler (1745–1804) was the first person in Britain to fly. He achieved the feat in a hot air balloon, taking off from Edinburgh on 25 August 1784, several weeks ahead of his aviation rival Vincenzo Lunardi, whose first flight (in a hydrogen balloon) took place in London on 15 September 1784. During the flight, Tytler only managed to rise a couple of metres from the ground; but two days later he made it to height of 30 metres and travelled roughly 1 kilometre.

Samuel Franklin Cody (1867–1913) made the first officially recognised aeroplane flight in the UK. On 16 October 1908 his 'British Army Aeroplane No.1' took off from Farnborough Airport, Hampshire. He flew for 426 metres at an altitude of 5.5 metres. The flight lasted thirty seconds, and the super-flimsy aircraft was damaged during landing. Cody (a fame-seeker who borrowed his name from 'Buffalo' Bill Cody and claimed to be his son) was killed during an even less successful flight on 7 August 1913.

Three British kings — but which was the only one to speak English?

William I • Richard I • George I

ANSWER: Whilst none of them spoke English when they came to the throne, George I was the only one who eventually mastered it.

William the Conqueror (1028–87) spoke Norman French as his first language, and his courtly language was French. He never mastered English. In those days, the native tongue of the island consisted of various dialects of Old English, as spoken by the Anglo-Saxons. The influence of Norman and French on this ancestral language resulted in Middle English, the London-based version (disseminated and immortalised by the writer Geoffrey Chaucer in later centuries) being far more recognisably 'English' than its predecessor.

Richard the Lionheart (1157–99) had little incentive to master the language of his English-speaking subjects, spending most of his life in Normandy and the Holy Land. Although born in Oxford, Richard was an infrequent visitor to England as an adult. He returned briefly in 1194 after being released from the cells of the grudge-holding Duke of Austria. His release had looked highly unlikely, as the ransom required was equivalent to twice the annual revenue of the Crown of England; but somehow the cash was stumped up, and Richard went back to England to be crowned for a second time, to show everyone that he was still in the game.

George I (1660–1727) was largely unloved in Britain, the fact that he did not speak English being one of many reasons. The English court and its onion-like layers of associated aristocrats had been British-with-a-large-pinch-of-French for so long that the sudden arrival of German offended conservative sensibilities. George did learn English later in his reign, however, and the succeeding four Georges were raised speaking English as a second language, along with German (French still being the official courtly tongue).

Three invasions of Britain, one of which failed to get a single man to shore — but which?

The Battle of Stamford Bridge
• The Spanish Armada •
The Battle of Fishguard

ANSWER: The Spanish Armada.

At **the Battle of Stamford Bridge**, 25 September 1066, Anglo-Saxon-Danish King Harold II (Godwinson) defeated Norwegian invaders led by King Harald Hardrada of Norway and Harold's brother Tostig Godwinson. The latter two were both killed; but the battle, although a victory for the English army, had big repercussions. Harold's men had to ride back south and face another invading force in the shape of William, Duke of Normandy. This led to the Battle of Hastings, an arrow in the eye and, 900 years later, W.C. Sellar and R.J. Yeatman's perennial classic *1066 And All That*.

The **Spanish Armada**, sighted on 19 July 1588, was famously dispersed by the combined forces of appalling weather and Sir Francis Drake.

The **Battle of Fishguard** lasted from 22 to 24 February 1797. The invaders were French – fresh from revolution – led by Irish-American Colonel William Tate, masterminded by General Lazare Hoche and supported by the Irish Republicans of Wolfe Tone. The plan was scuppered by a combination of bad organisation and bad weather (the bulk of the forces were due to land in Ireland, but were delayed by conditions at sea). Approximately 1,400 men landed at Fishguard, and there was a spot of looting before a troop of 500 defenders arrived under the command of John Campbell, 1st Baron Cawdor. After a minor skirmish Tate surrendered, folklore maintaining that Welsh women in traditional red cloaks, mistaken for British Grenadiers, had routed the invaders. The Battle of Fishguard marked the last attempted land invasion in Britain.

The ghost of a historical figure haunts all three of these sites. Who is it — and which is the only place where it appears with its head on its shoulders?

The Tower of London • Hampton Court Palace • Blickling Hall

ANSWER: All are haunted by the ghost of Anne Boleyn, second wife of King Henry VIII. Hampton Court is the only site where she never appears without her head.

The **Tower of London** has all manner of ghosts from various centuries. Anne sometimes manifests in the Chapel of St Peter ad Vincula, although she prefers wandering al fresco. She was beheaded here and occasionally, as Stanley Holloway once sang, 'With her head tucked underneath her arm, she walks the Bloody Tower'. There are all manner of stories, including sentries who have tried to bayonet her, and others who have seen whole Tudor parties progressing towards the place where she was executed.

Hampton Court Palace's version of Anne wears a blue dress and walks slowly down the corridors looking terribly sad. It's difficult to guess what her response might be to the other two of the six wives who haunt here – melancholy Jane Seymour and the screaming Catherine Howard, perpetually fleeing from the swordsman who is about to cut off her head.

Blickling Hall in Norfolk was Anne's childhood home. Every year on 19 May, the anniversary of her death, she hurtles down the long drive in a coach drawn by six headless horses, topped off with a headless coachman. Decapitated Anne sits within, dressed in white, her severed head in her lap. Upon reaching the front door, the coach vanishes, and Anne spends the rest of the night a-haunting. To stretch the credulity of even the most avid ghost watcher, her headless father and brother haunt here too.

For the record, Anne also haunts Hever Castle in Kent (the Boleyn's family seat), Windsor Castle and Marwell Hall (now part of Marwell Zoo) in Hampshire.

Three criminals famous for the same thing — but what is it?

Jack Sheppard • Alfie Hinds • Ronald Biggs

ANSWER: All three won celebrity by escaping from prison – but only Biggs was never recaptured.

Alfie Hinds' (1917–91) first experience behind bars was in 1953, arrested for robbery and sentenced to twelve years in Nottingham Prison. Sneaking through locked doors and scaling a high wall, he escaped in 1955. Popularised as 'Houdini Hinds' in the press, he was recaptured 248 days later. He went on to escape from the law courts in London, although this latest liberty only lasted five hours. His third escape was from Chelmsford prison in 1957, after which he worked for two years as a used car dealer in Ireland under the pseudonym William Herbert Bishop. He ended up in Parkhurst Prison, and was finally released in 1966.

Jack Sheppard (1702–24) was the Alfie Hinds of his day, imprisoned five times in 1724 and liberating himself on four occasions. Robbery was his game, and his daring escapes made him a household name. His flame was bright and brief, and he was captured, tried and hanged at Tyburn in 1724. Fame had not finished with him, however: stories of his exploits continued to circulate, fuelled by the popular play *The Beggar's Opera* by John Gay (1728), in which the anti-hero Macheath was based on Sheppard. He returned to public consciousness following the publication of William Harrison Ainsworth's novel *Jack Sheppard* in 1840, and Macheath was later reborn in Berthold Brecht and Kurt Weill's twentieth-century *The Threepenny Opera*.

Ronald Biggs (1929–2013) was one of the men convicted for the Great Train Robbery in 1963. He was sentenced to twenty-four years in Wandsworth Prison, but escaped in 1965. He was never recaptured as such, living for thirty-six years in Australia and Brazil, avoiding extradition, and even appearing on a Sex Pistols record in 1978. In 2001 he voluntarily returned to the UK and was arrested, but was released eight years later on compassionate grounds.

Three men claim to have reached America first — but who is the only one with historical proof?

Richard Americk • Prince Madoc • St Brendan of Clonfert

ANSWER: All three have been put forward as the first Europeans to reach America, but only Richard Americk was involved in a voyage verified by historical records.

Richard Americk, or ap Meurig (1445–1503) was the principal funder of a ship that sailed beyond Iceland to discover new fishing grounds. Captained by John Cabot, the vessel hit America (Newfoundland) in 1497. However, legend maintains that they got there even earlier – sometime between 1479 and 1482, at least ten years before Columbus. Over the years writers have found Americk's name irresistible and put him forward as the source of 'America'. More sober consensus says that the continent was named in 1507 after Amerigo Vespucci, an Italian explorer and map-maker.

Prince Madoc was a member of the Welsh Royal Family, sailing west in 1170 and discovering America. According to legend, he and his brother Riryd set sail from Rhos-on-Sea, leading a fleet of would-be settlers. Making landfall, 100 men established a colony, while Madoc and the others returned to Wales, recruited more colonists and returned across the ocean. No more was ever heard of them; but legend, as ever, was undeterred. It is said that Madoc landed in either Florida or Alabama, and colonised from there, following river valleys into the Midwest. Evidence for this hinges on some Celtic-like hill forts, and some Welsh-soundalike words in the language of the Mandan Indians – said to be descendants of Madoc's people.

Sometime between the years AD 512 and 530 **St Brendan of Clonfert** (c. 484–c. 577) set sail from a spot near Ardfert in south-west Ireland. He was searching for Tír na nÓg, known as the Isle of Youth, the Isle of Delight, or the Isle of the Blessed. It took him seven years to get there, and the land he found was possibly one of the West Indies. None of this appears to have a foothold in the truth, sadly.

Image credits

PAGE 3
Bellew, Hawkins and Drake. (THP)

PAGE 5
Anne Hathaway's house, Stratford-upon-Avon. (Library of Congress, LC-DIG-ppmsc-08873)

PAGE 7
Tending the moustache. (THP)

PAGE 9
Churchill and Stalin in 1945. (Library of Congress, LC-USZ62-7449)

PAGE 9
President John F. Kennedy. (Library of Congress, LC-USZ61-1173)

PAGE 11
Highwaymen at work, as pictured by an early edition of the *Newgate Calendar*. (THP)

PAGE 13
German spies are listening! (Poster from 1918, Library of Congress, LC-USZC4-2793)

PAGE 15
A disastrous fire on London Bridge! The wooden structure burning down in 1758. (THP)

PAGE 17
A bear. (THP)

PAGE 19
Kings John, Edward I and James I. (THP)

PAGES 21 AND 23
(Chris West)

PAGE 25
The famous Stamford knocker, stolen from Oxford University in 1333. (With thanks to Simon Garbutt)

PAGE 25
Wokingham Town Hall. (THP)

PAGE 25
Tutbury Castle viewed from within the keep, looking west. (With thanks to Dave Harris)

PAGE 27
The royal coat of arms. (THP)

PAGE 29
Henry VI. (THP)

PAGE 29
Charles I. (THP)

PAGE 29
Robert Grosseteste, from the window of St Paul's parish church, Morton, near Gainsborough. (THP)

PAGE 31
Henry VIII. (THP)

PAGE 31

Oliver Cromwell. (THP)

PAGE 31

Margaret Thatcher. (Library of Congress, LC-DIG-ppmsc-03266)

PAGE 33

Assassination of Spencer Perceval. (THP)

PAGE 33

Lord Kitchener. (Library of Congress, LC-USZC4-11015)

PAGE 33

Lord and Lady Mountbatten. (Library of Congress, LC-DIG-ggbain-35008)

PAGE 35

Lambert Simnel. (THP)

PAGE 37

'Ich Dien', meaning 'I serve', the symbol and motto of the Prince of Wales since the time of the Black Prince.

PAGE 39

Lady Randolph Churchill. (Library of Congress, LC-DIG-ggbain-14381)

PAGE 39

The last published photograph of Edward VII, seen here with the soon-to-be-King George and the then-Prince Edward.

PAGE 39

Nelson. (THP)

PAGE 41

The noose… (THP)

PAGE 43

Saints alive! (THP)

PAGE 45

Plesiosaurus dolichodeirus from Conybeare's 1824 paper that described an almost complete plesiosaur skeleton found by Mary Anning in 1823. (*Transactions of the Geological Society of London*, 1824)

PAGE 45

Ichthyosaur communis. (*Transactions of the Geological Society of London*, 1824)

PAGE 45

A young *pterodactylus antiquus*. (THP)

PAGE 47

Soldiers of the First World War. (Katie Beard)

PAGE 49

A policeman. (THP)

PAGE 51

Agecroft Hall – in its new location! (Library of Congress, LC-DIG-csas-06502)

PAGE 51

London Bridge. (Library of Congress, LC-USZ62-133248)

PAGE 51

Belle Tout Lighthouse. (With thanks to robef)

PAGE 53
A headless chalk outline. (THP)

PAGE 55
Clumber Park chapel. (With thanks to Wayne Austin)

PAGE 55
Costessey Hall. (THP)

PAGE 55
High Head Castle. (THP)

PAGE 57
Guy Fawkes. (THP)

PAGE 57
Florence Nightingale. (Library of Congress, LC-U5262-5877)

PAGE 57
King Alfred. (THP)

PAGE 59
Detail of a pirate. (Library of Congress, LC-U5ZC2-5494)

PAGE 61
The death of Wat Tyler during the Peasants' Revolt. (THP)

PAGE 63
Hunting the Mallard. (THP)

PAGE 65
Quartered body. (Library of Congress, LC-U5262-77668)

PAGE 67
Victorian hot chocolate. (THP)

PAGE 69
Queen Victoria. (Library of Congress, LC-U5262-93417)

PAGE 71
Pict. (THP)

PAGE 73
Stonehenge. (THP)

PAGE 75
Slave's back (Library of Congress, LC-U5262-98515)

PAGE 75
Bull. (THP)

PAGE 75
'Tortures of the training room'. (Library of Congress, LC-U5262-57341)

PAGE 77
Churchill. (THP)

PAGE 79
10 Downing Street. (Sergeant Tom Robinson RLC RLC/MOD, licensed under the Open Government Licence v2.0, http://www.defenceimagery.mod.uk)

PAGE 81
Diplodocus. (With thanks to Dmitry Bogdanov (dmitrchel@mail.ru), http://creativecommons.org/licenses/by/3.0)

If you enjoyed this book, you may also be interested in…

The Secret History of Oxford

PAUL SULLIVAN

Filled with hundreds of facts and anecdotes, this book reveals Oxford's amusing, unlikely and downright wonderful history. For example, did you know that the founder of Oxford was eaten by wolves, or that one of the Fellows of Christ Church was a bear?

978 0 7524 9956 7

Zombies from History

GEOFF HOLDER

Are you worried about the zombie apocalypse? Well, fret no more! With full zombie-hunting details – including the locations of tombs, any wounds and weaknesses and a carefully calculated difficulty rating – this book assesses some of history's most famous names, and tells you what to do if they try to eat your face.

978 0 7524 9964 2

Bloody British History: Oxford

PAUL SULLIVAN

The first historical record of Oxford laments that the city had been burnt to the ground by Vikings. Its students were poverty-stricken desperados in perpetual armed conflict with the townsmen. One of its principal colleges, meanwhile, doubled as a slaughterhouse. Paul Sullivan explores the history the town doesn't want you to know!

978 0 7524 6549 4

Visit our website and discover thousands of other History Press books.

www.thehistorypress.co.uk